D0394481

This book belongs to

norman rockwell

THE

Wit & Humor

OF

NORMAN ROCKWELL

———

ARIEL BOOKS

ANDREWS AND McMEEL

KANSAS CITY

Frontispiece: FRAMED
Saturday Evening Post cover,
March 2, 1946

Book design by Susan Hood

THE

Wit & Humor

OF

NORMAN ROCKWELL

THE BODY BUILDER

—

Saturday Evening Post cover
April 29, 1922

BEDSIDE MANNER

Saturday Evening Post cover
March 10, 1923

THE CRITIC

—

Saturday Evening Post cover
July 21, 1928

THE PIE THIEF

—

Saturday Evening Post cover
August 18, 1928

SERENADE

Saturday Evening Post cover
September 22, 1928

THE GOSSIPS

—

Saturday Evening Post cover
January 12, 1929

TRAVELER

———

Saturday Evening Post cover
July 13, 1929

NO SWIMMING

—

Saturday Evening Post cover
June 15, 1929

JAZZ IT UP

———

Saturday Evening Post cover
November 2, 1929

PRACTICING

Saturday Evening Post cover
November 7, 1931

CHILD PSYCHOLOGY

Saturday Evening Post cover
November 25, 1933

HANG ON!

Saturday Evening Post cover
July 13, 1935

THE NANNY

Saturday Evening Post cover
October 24, 1936

SEE THE WORLD

Saturday Evening Post cover
April 24, 1937

DOLORES AND EDDIE

―

Saturday Evening Post cover
June 12, 1937

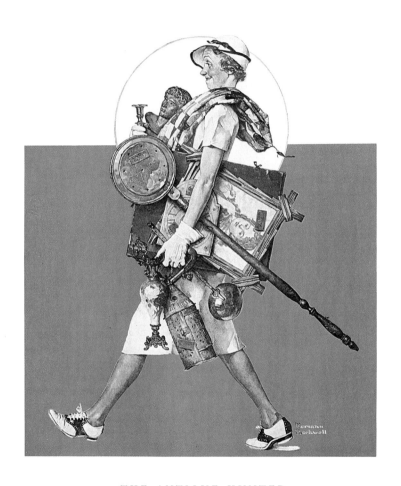

THE ANTIQUE HUNTER

Saturday Evening Post cover
July 31, 1937

WET PAINT!

Saturday Evening Post cover
October 2, 1937

FIRE!

Saturday Evening Post cover
May 27, 1944

THE JESTERS

Saturday Evening Post cover
February 11, 1939

THE SPORTING LIFE

Saturday Evening Post cover
April 29, 1939

SHERIFF AND PRISONER

———

Saturday Evening Post cover
November 4, 1939

THE WORKS!

Saturday Evening Post cover
May 18, 1940

SCHOOLGIRL

—

Saturday Evening Post cover
March 1, 1941

THANKSGIVING DAY

———

Saturday Evening Post cover
November 28, 1942

PLAYING CHECKERS

Saturday Evening Post cover
April 3, 1943

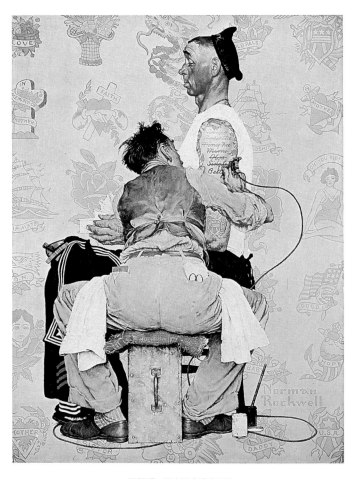

THE TATOOIST

—

Saturday Evening Post cover
March 4, 1944

APRIL FOOL'S

—

Saturday Evening Post cover
March 31, 1945

THE HAPPY GARDENER

—

Saturday Evening Post cover
March 22, 1947

BABYSITTING

———

Saturday Evening Post cover
November 8, 1947

THE DIETER

———

Saturday Evening Post cover
January 3, 1953

FEEDING TIME

Saturday Evening Post cover
January 9, 1954

A FAIR CATCH

Saturday Evening Post cover
August 20, 1955

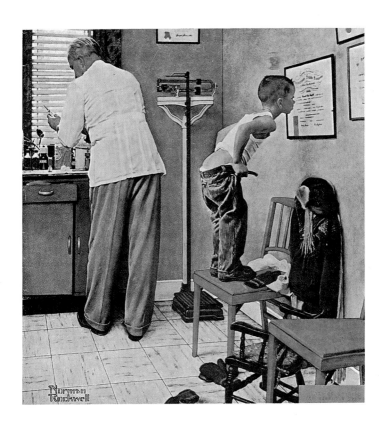

AT THE DOCTOR'S

Saturday Evening Post cover
March 15, 1958